Peace of (Mind) Moments

Sammantha Rials

In Dedication to

my beautiful mother,

hard-working father

and

kind brother.

Sealofters Press, Inc.
1061 East Indiantown Rd, Suite #104
Jupiter, FL 33477

Sealofters Press, Inc. was established in 2008 as a publishing alternative to the large, commercial publishing houses currently dominating the book publishing industry. Sealofters Press, Inc. is committed to publishing works of educational, cultural and community value.

Contents

Wanting and Loving

You or I

Should I paint the flower?

Would it be beautiful and resemble the rose?

No it's a lily.

I'm imagining things again.

It would be nice to be that breathtaking.

I'm jealous.

The beauty could never be foreseen.

Of a seed.

How dumbfounded were those pilgrims when it smelled of sweet essence.

Were they as jealous as I am now?

No.

I would think not.

There would be no reason to be.

Survival: The intention to keep a story up and live to tell it.

If I were in a life or death situation I would survive.

No doubt.

Carrying water can't be that hard.

Fishing.

Taking away a bear's meal.

That would challenge any human.

Who actually wants to kill something.

Too foul…

For me.

But, I'm me.

Oh god.

Hope the lily sees it's me.

Knows I'm pure.

I swear.

Not dying with sins.

Overrated.

Sorry, Satan.

Wait for the worshipers.

They're coming.

No denying that.

Good luck.

You'll be against me.

I'm one tough cookie.

Don't be discouraged.

It's all in the head.

I would know.

People want to be me… I want to be them… Debating.

How about deciding?

It's not that hard to agree that your name is yours.

Go get the birth certificate.

See the family photo albums.

It's you.

Who else can claim those memories?

Remember, not everything can be yours.

All of the things already are.

They are yours.

Don't let yourself take pity on the prayer you once had to gain all that you lost.

Now you've got it.

Take the money and run.

Run where money can't be found.

Hide it.

Crucify the crop that craved human worthiness.

Because you're already worthy of it all.

Eventually Eternal

How you crave the desire,

to want,

more than you feel.

To love,

more than you are capable.

To track a ghost,

whose pale figure

steps ups to the plate

when asked of fate.

A miracle,

with a feeling of doubt.

Nothing

will come out.

Surprise your eyes,

you won't see it.

But the catch,

like you're hanging

off the edge of another world.

Yet something is left behind,

it's you,

lifting your conscious

above the level of time.

Transcending into the

moments of purity.

Where with no glasses,

we can visualize

each and every

inch of the

other and grasp it with both

hands.

While not letting it fall away,

because it isn't even there.

A mere figment of what once was,

and always will be

something so pure, it stays engraved in history.

Addictive Insanity

Creating you was hard.

It was painful to rebuild that illegal substance that your brain had inherited.

The part that bothered my heart was that I gave it to you.

Your whole world was encased with me and I was trapped in your head.

Theoretically, I couldn't move from that space.

Mindless mistakes cause unintentional hatred.

Which, I in turn, slap you in the face with.

You ruined the idea of happiness and freedom for me.

Whoever said I needed it though?

Maybe this whole scheme broke an uneven plan I had developed out of pain.

A pure and unnatural animation of a life.

But I helped you forget your own.

As much as you had killed my calamity of a scene for some movie,

I loved it.

You had me hooked on a pill of enzymes only I could take.

My body was immune to your hyper-active tension.

Probably because I intensified those tendencies.

I understand that the world I made for you was perfect.

But the dynamic of you furnishing my realistic memories enthralled me,

for every wrong reason.

To be honest, after some time, I don't even know why I stayed,

stayed within reach of you.

I believe I needed it,

I liked the pain,

I like the capacity of love you had for me.

Yes But No

I can feel it again. The small strokes you take and the smile that instigates more sensuality. You're leading me on and somehow I don't mind. Maybe that is because I feel your heart when you are nowhere near. It's falling out of the sky and lifting bright lights. I see your pretty eyes and feel so much emotion. It all tastes so sweet, so personal. As much as it isn't real, I beg to you that it is. I know that I am more than some album in a phone to you or even a "first choice", because you wouldn't even pick me at all. You don't want anybody or anything to tie you down but you feel connected to me and oddly enough, I do to you.

Psychoanalysis

That docile little chameleon,

unable to help himself.

Independent.

So relatively simple to read.

Yet at times very difficult to read,

never unimaginable in your eyes.

Everything was a challenge

for me

to hold back my urges,

to tell you that I knew

you hurt

and weren't up for

an immediate class in psychology.

This meaning,

you did not fully get how you felt.

The enigmatic

little angel

who craved a side of hell.

In a sense,

the real world

at it's hardest.

Not a hellion,

knowing what you want

was a strong point.

Getting there,

that needed practice.

Vulnerable Intimacy

I could feel my own hand shaking. It mixed with the melodic hum of your heart beat. I was cold and damp in my hair. On the contrary, every part of you was warm. A part of me was jealous of your independence in that area. I needed your body to keep me from freezing to death. Sounds odd, but I actually loved needing someone; needing you, for once. I loved having that dependence on someone.

You would look at me and I'd just sort of pass all of my tension away. That is because you gave me attention. And the pure emotion was salved with everything but negligence and pain. We were both so pleased by the way we slowly became intertwined. Nobody was far away, but it remained only us. That meant more to me than you could ever know. Simply because, despite how close we were, there was still a sense of loneliness.

Losing and Hurting

Gone, Gone

Do you not see my dear?

That the light, inside me

is no longer here?

It has been removed,

my thoughts have

become less and less

mine.

And the words I speak

come out

without my own tone of voice.

I am beginning

to miss who I am very much.

As well as who I was

before I gave in

to premature love

and the idea that a solid emotion saves you.

The things you do not feel create you,

not what you do.

I let myself go when I felt instant happiness.

That isn't how to become

what you want.

I thought anything would change just

like that.

It didn't.

I fell even deeper,

not into a hole.

I'm actually worldlier

now.

Other worldly things can't touch me at the moment.

Because I'm not on the brink anymore.

I am deep down,

into the dirt.

Regret

Don't make me wait for you to say it.

Don't let me say it over and over

unless you do not understand.

Please believe me when I smile and laugh at what we used to be.

I honestly do not mind that we are no longer

what that was.

All that it could have been.

Don't get me wrong, I loved every bit of it.

But I am at a new part of my life

now.

Though I will not pretend I didn't love you once.

Or that some part of me will always

be drawn to you.

I still am.

The "maybes"

and the "do's"

and the "don'ts".

That list still applies to our relationship.

Perhaps it always will.

I wouldn't guess against it.

Things have changed,

I have,

and along with that,

so have you.

Timeless & Useless

One more time.

Sing that song.

I will cry.

Sob.

Listen.

We need another bonding experience.

I lacked too many with you.

Besides, we finally have time.

No more rush.

And look, the exact clock I started the day we met went off when the world started.

Realistically, you stopped time for me.

In your own life.

I caused you to shut up and listen.

Because the pull I had on you was hard and my grasp was rough.

It left marks.

The ones that I adore.

They are phenomenal.

I changed you.

Even physically.

The rest of you was in stone.

Hopefully you can turn into medusa and freeze my persona as well.

Anyway, let me keep wishing.

You don't seem to want to listen.

Sorry I took forever.

I thought there was longer.

Prints

You showed me exactly what I do not want. The pain you do feel is experimental and toyed with by others as you do the same to them. Why is that around me you hide from who we both know you are? That outer shell didn't take too long to break and when it did... there on the pavement I walk on, is you. I physically walk all over you. Meaning that the soles of my feet walk on the heavy imprints you made. If I am not mistaken, everything or at least most things do rise. So these footprints could travel up to my heart or lodge themselves in my brain stem, theoretically speaking. I say this as though you haven't already done something to that part of my body. I couldn't tell you why certain people connect while other people spend their lives wrapped close to each other, never feeling any real spark. Needless to say, you make your mark on someone because they see you for what you are, and that's both the best and worst thing. I will, until the day I die, love you for the things you did for me and the messages you pressed into my bones. The least I can do is hope that some pieces of me are in you.

Sammantha Rials

Unending

I'd love to say

that my mind never wanders back to him,

but that would be far from true.

I gave a lot, without being given what I deserved

in return.

That could be a reminder.

That was fair; hurts regardless.

I missed him for too long.

Almost in a way that took,

took from my soul,

and bled me out.

Because I had no way to stop myself

from giving my power away.

Only in the hope that if I held on to the thought of him,

he would hold on to the thought of me.

In this, letting go was a frequent struggle.

I would not let myself.

I had way too much fear.

It was just tugging on me,

27

constantly hurting.

I did whatever I could,

and still do

to forget.

Need Answers

I know that one day I will know,

know that you loved me.

I will know how much it took for you not to admit it

and to know why you wouldn't tell me the truth.

Perhaps I do already know some of these questions.

But for old time sake, let's say that I have no clue.

Would you tell me everything if I asked?

Could you give me that much?

You do realize that if I knew, there would be no more guessing.

It would be great.

I wouldn't need to guess how you do this all without me…

Or why you look at me so strangely.

There would be no problem when I told you to come closer.

Because, by then, I would be allowed in.

I mean, you could not even guess how many times you would show up

just so I could get a glimpse of you.

I would have given my happiness away,

to see you smile.

That ruined me.

You would never have given me a hand.

At a Time

You are so strong and independent. All the creativity that made you an artist has also inspired the serious, livid experimentation that I was so eagerly involved in. A sense of pleasure and average contentment came from my experiences with you. I still have times where I lay awake and think of the talks we would have at dusk about people watching and how we analyzed practical minded people vs. the daydreamers. You were always more of a daydreamer stuck in a practical body. You told me I was subtle in the way I went about anything I did, not unrealistic, but not too far fetched. We both had no idea how others perceived us. Over time I have realized how amazing it is that we had such knowledge of the other. It faded with time but we still know parts of the other that most people wouldn't. I know you tell me way too little compared to how you feel; now I just wonder where the words went.

Misconception

You told me that I was crazy.

You admitted to having some odd attraction

to me.

You created a lie that we would all live through.

You stopped my life and I am hoping that I can get back into the ignition and

jump it again.

You had me by the first conversation when I realized you cared.

You never actually let me in

on why you wanted to know me

inside and out.

You smiled way too much around me.

You were the one,

the one that filled my glass. When you dropped it,

I was made to pick up the glass.

To this day, I still cannot drink out of it properly or

put all the pieces back together.

You scarred by burning.

You seeped through my persona so quickly.

You know me.

My name.

Why I hurt.

How insecure I happen to be.

The soft spots that I cover up

with cheap makeup.

The days I feel the worst.

The shirts that bring back way too many memories.

The people I love.

The creations I piece together in my head.

The secrets,

that I don't even know about myself.

You caught me off guard.

You stole everything and left me with no satisfaction.

You mauled the poor, little prostitute.

You deceived the baby deer.

You turned into a beast.

And switched my part as Belle, to the lady who tends to you

on only some accounts.

Thank you,

for downgrading me.

Way Back, All Along

You loved me.

I let you go as far into me as you could possibly go,

physically and emotionally.

No connection,

in the entire world I've known,

has ever compared.

The only topper,

the day you told me it wasn't love anymore.

The day I knew it had become lust and nothing more.

We had switched places,

in that moment I knew how you had felt,

from the beginning.

Now I, myself

am very sorry.

Stir Me Up

See, you and I messed up a long time ago. Before we met we had hurt ourselves. We had fluctuated between substances and relished in all aftermath. Nobody could fill the void that either of us had sunk into the depths of our minds. Mindlessness can lead to becoming agnostic and idiotic, but it is painless. You don't have to feel enough to actually get sad; it's like floating. Floating through without any attachment. When you have become desensitized and then given the permission to really feel, anything gets under your skin. You got under my skin the moment I met you. The exact moment I saw you. Something made my head spin and to the point that I actually liked it. I don't understand it too much yet.

Him

Weighted heavily on persuasion and faithfully by religion, he stepped right out of the path that would have led him directly to me. Perhaps for all the most intent reasoning that meant he would lose if he gained. But that's the contradiction. I can blame nobody but myself. I push until I can pull back manually. See, I want control and that means I am uncomfortable with anybody who I become reluctantly dependent upon. A fear resonates in the pit of my heart when I hear him say my name. For I am sure that one day... that inflection won't match the pronunciation of my name and be replaced by the passion of somebody he knows loves him and wants to trust themselves in the hopes that he possibly means more than anything. I, at one point believed exactly how incredible he was. But I forgot. And with temporary amnesia, would never again fully love the idiot of the person, who tried their best with me. Messed with, I am the classically disturbed character with a major tragic flaw. Maybe the indirect fear of missing out creates my indifference to act on the purest of emotions. Whatever the fact may be, I resent myself kind of for screwing him over. I'm not sure I hurt him. But I am clear that when he aimlessly asks me how I am, I'm on his mind, even more than the sands of time. Backtracking, because I am the one with whom he regresses. We knew each other, maybe that's it. Regardless, I know that this time we won't have to come back again. Between him and I, the time may remain as still as the air.

Something There

I cannot manifest that feeling under anybody else's presence. I may feel a slight twinge when they say my name or ask me a question. None the less, with you I feel things with my whole heart. I mean *all* of it faints and for a temporary moment my conscious allows for a breather. This does not animate enough to let me love… But I do get a taste. Dismembered from my brain, my emotions just swell up. I couldn't even tell you how I feel if you asked, but it hurts a lot. The pain is the type that almost gives you a jolt though, the kind that reminds you you're alive. I know right now, it isn't going to work… But I am going on to much more. So are you. Down the road, I want to meet you. That is, if I can. Maybe I'll have had experienced that feeling come exactly the same ten thousand more times. Or maybe, it will just be gone.

Leave, But Stay

I watched people and I watched you. How you walked, talked and grimaced. Even the way you smirked. I watched behind every intention. You were this enigma. I fell in love with this amazing person who had a facade even bigger than his heart. I could feel you ache, I could hear you scream, I could hear you feel. The best was your moan, not always in pleasure, but in breaks. Because I knew I was your escape and you were able to leave yourself with me. I was shelter for you and when you tumbled, I tumbled. When we both tumbled, it was catastrophic. I wanted that. To be the mess of a person who had layers of themselves. And with you, I had this beautiful mess of a young soul. I wish, with a lot of me, that I had the heart to hate you. In reality, I have so much more to give to you than hate. You made me happier and full and I carry you with me. I can do anything with my life and I very well will be with somebody else, but I have this imprint of you and I love that no matter what, I know that what we had was real. I know that nobody can take my first love from me. I will never give up on finding myself and what makes me believe in all that I am. You did, whenever I could not. I love you enough to make you proud as well.

I'm OK with It

I'm acceptant that you do love her. You always have loved her. All I wanted was for that passion to all together dissolve for most years of my life. One of the strongest emotions I have ever developed and felt is envy; the envy I had toward her. I wanted you, almost as much as a cat wants to scratch a post. It would have been fun to ruin you…But now I have enough knowledge to enable that urge to be held back.

I used to dream about having what you two have. Not necessarily being her, but becoming and taking the place of that energy and all that it held with it. In all honesty, I imagined that you adored me, even more than you do her.

Watching the way you two interact is still painful. I'm by far over the tactics I used to have. I don't confront you on the advantages of choosing me. I won't deny that you love her anymore.

Tell Me It Gets Better

I miss it all, even the parts of it that I hated, most of the time. Every single part of me holds the memories of being with you. Not that I'm not anyway, just I'm way more alone and these hallways have too many damn voices to decipher. I wouldn't even say that I have flashbacks; my body just aches when I think for a long amount of time. I can't find enough time to even express or detail in words how much my life altered upon meeting you. Nothing was as bland, and I took it upon myself to finally feel and hone in on that muscle in myself. For the longest time, I absorbed matters from such a slight, casual perspective. I wouldn't allow myself to genuinely feel without filtering it through a scale of whether or not I deserved it. What I did was shut out a mass amount of opportunities, which I don't regret at all. I know without an ounce of doubt, that if I had kept on pushing you away that I'd dig myself in a hole that would take years to get out of. I mean maybe I convinced myself to let it all go, every second of our exchanges. The reality is that I didn't, my mind wouldn't allow it.

Sort of Revenge

I want to cut you

and have it hurt.

Hurt like a burn.

A branding mark with my initials.

You always said I was a cow.

I remember all of those comments.

And they have scarred me.

Look at all my scars and tell me that

you didn't make them.

All of them.

I would beg for you to apologize.

But I doubt you would ever

admit to any of those emotional threats and assaults.

Although they're imprinted in me.

Stained in my subconscious mind.

In a way that is irremovable.

Not even the strongest

remedy could fix me.

Prescriptions would make it worse.

I'm uncertified in medical fields

to even prescribe or analyze a particular

condition.

If I have anything,

well,

wrong with me.

What I don't understand

is how we could possibly determine the human analogy

of something so wrong

within us

as one.

We can't be that in touch.

For Reference

I had to leave

if this hurt...

I was partially

intent on reminding

you

of my bittersweet sorrow.

I'm not sure

how much is left of me.

The depression remains.

The full glass I was born with,

spilled.

You were my replacement

Eventually the original,

it must come back.

I decided that should be before

I lean in too fast and

stop

so

slow

the light I used to see

is engulfed by the

dark

in relativity,

obviously.

Don't call me,

don't try to find me,

don't accidentally run into me.

Just remember but don't

let the nostalgia take over.

Promise me,

I am gone now and you know that.

Just Missing, & Wanting

I guess a lot of things change crazy suddenly. I didn't really expect this to happen. I couldn't have told you how I would react or how I'd feel but I know now that I've never had such a depth of love and care for someone in my life. I can't tell you how much I yearn to simply be with you. I mean this in the most innocent of terms. I want to see and touch your sweet face and tell you about my day. I don't need much more. I mean I do, but that's greedy. In basic terms, if I could have anything, it would be the knowledge that things will become similar to how they were once before. That maybe someday we can reunite and go to the springs and love on each other like we did before. I miss that real sensation I got with you. It was like I was on a high.

Per Say

This is my proposal, totally metaphoric.

One day, not so far off, I will be the old woman walking into a grocery store, hoping to get a smile from an oncoming stranger. The things worrying me now won't even be a second thought. My mind will be depleting away but my heart swelling with all of the love I now know, the world will be so much brighter and quite possibly even more unending and confusing. Maybe by then I will have found even more about what I do not know. I will have lost enough to realize that not everything is supposed to end up staying. I will have finally seen the ways in which everything turns out okay, somehow. Quite possibly I will have even been able to really fully let go of some things, even things that bother me now. I think that no matter what, my biggest hope is that by that time, I will have found faith in the divine order of all things, and how they do eventually add up.

Where I'd Want to Be

In some parallel universe, maybe we did end up together. I believe that all people come across each other in order to shape the other and bring them down the road they are going on. You brought me into a brand new road, the same one you had made yourself and as dark and scary as it got at times, your road had the best views. I was always infatuated with it all each and every time you drove me down it. I had this whole idea about where it would take us. The huge twist was that it slowly became a dead end, and when we stopped, we both idled. I don't exactly know where you went or if you drove back down it again, but I did. I drove it back, very slowly. All of the same milestones and geography were still there but they didn't stir me up in the same way, it was all bland. Even to this day some things still are, just because I had assumed I would never leave a road if you were not on it with me. I do, absolutely love driving on my own now but I do still come across the times where I wish it was still you and I, reading our own map.

Falling All The Way

The only person I know you to be is faltering. And I am painfully scared that we are becoming foreign to each other. Not that I have drastically changed, but I won't claim to be the same person that I was years ago. That could never be, way too much evolves day by day. It's all timing, I feel like then, at that point, we were perfect for each other. I heard once that sometimes things are so good that you almost have to break them in order to see it all a new. Brad Pitt said something like that in Fight Club. The whole idea sounds a little maniacal but the reality is that we sabotage most things. I do, probably more than I even realize. Maybe we think we have it too good. Somewhere in the back of our mind, it clicks that we must make it all blow up, just to feel something more. The human mind just messes with you. I remember when it was so easy to be happy, but now I see that I love the thick, heavy things that come with a sense of feeling lost. I think the waves of whatever we feel can sometimes ground us more than the actual ground itself.

Thinking

With Time

I don't believe that growing up means losing who you are, but rather finding what looks and feels good on you, regardless of what anyone else tells you. There are circumstances that force you to battle with the deepest elements in yourself. Things come up out of pure need for growth and experience, so that we can become what we are potentially destined to be. What we are meant to be, although, is ever changing. There is no end to what we will become. I have heard countless people recount that the times they thought they had figured everything out, were the times when something happened to prove that the exact opposite was true. Maybe there are ironies and they overlap all of the coincidences, but I am not positive. Especially, because as much as some things make sense to me, there are things that still do not. You both love and despise certain people, all because of their power to control how and what you feel. But you may be self-confident and respect yourself and yet still let yourself be dictated. There, you begin to see such hypocrisy. Why do we pick those that temper our love for ourselves and make us insecure? Is it growing up when you find that you are quite capable of finding and choosing someone who actually reflects the good in yourself back to you?

Not Math

Spoken through lingual tongue.

Spit from years of denial.

Admit to the wrong doing.

All will fall back into place.

Relish from the man that gave you up.

Guffaw at the miniature smile.

It's the end.

Such a wait.

Sitting in a sought out plan.

Unable to sink your feet in.

Quite possibly... Buried.

Already minded enough to spill.

Fan it all out, into the lights that cascade all.

Unleash the wolves that prey.

Sharks that smell.

Lava that burns.

Sing for the choir.

Death ridden, they become melancholy and see the truth.

That all remains,

times…Times…

Whatever number you choose.

Magnify the potential and,

the product becomes your own.

Left, Right, Wrong, Right

I know you realize I won't come.

I am not going to show.

You have known that forever.

Is hope easier to trust than knowledge?

Pretty debatable.

Maybe even stumping.

But,

I choose hope... theoretically.

Reality and experience would lead me

to believe that knowledge raises potential for success.

Success rates are low in general.

Although.

It all depends on who you are talking to,

perception overrides almost anything.

The key phenomena is individuality.

It almost holds those phenomenal life secrets.

That nobody actually knows about.

One of the most basic human diseases has to be

the wanting to know,

everything.

We all want to understand,

to comprehend.

We get enough though,

we have emotion.

Look, K(no)w a Man

Sarcasm.

My great humanitarian,

who used a form,

in a way like literature.

Breaking apart the negative,

from the positive.

Creating an undeniable humor,

even in the dullest moments.

The people who

don't understand

take the reality check

to heart.

Feasting their eyes

only upon what it is

they see,

physically at most.

Relying on the solemn,

to remind their

positive deeds.

Realize

At some point you will have a moment,

when it comes from a good place, and you will see the full circle.

It will make sense.

All of the little things will be big again

and all of the hurt will flare back up into you

but it will also disappear.

Something will finally click,

there are certain people who are meant to go,

instances that go better in your head,

situations that would not have been better if you told the truth,

and times where the worst possible experience actually saved you,

from something far, far worse.

It won't be soon but it won't be later than the time that will serve you best.

Not all that we want is from a place of need or knowing,

If it turned out how we wanted,

there wouldn't even be a happily ever after.

Happy comes from acceptance and knowledge of what is supposed to be,

not the want for more.

Enough?

We want more,

we always want more,

more love,

more happy,

more authentic,

more of what feeds us.

And whatever that is

begins to simply ruin our lives.

Regardless of what we make,

create, and ruin in our life

one thing stands alone,

how we leave the things we made.

May it be an empire,

a beautiful child,

a railroad track,

or even a little old house with a cake you stole from

some cute little store.

The point is that

we just leave and in that,

73

we have the things that stay behind,

and that is about all.

It isn't possible,

to document or paint a picture

of someone else's enigmatic presence

and being.

Nobody can perfectly

describe how it is to hold hands,

or feel the skin and look into the

eyes of another person they care

so greatly for.

You want it,

to know that feeling

where someone cares so much.

Like listening to an old man

talk about his late wife

about her life,

(and you imagine) her joy and light

in his eyes.

That real admiration,

you want that,

you want more.

Explanation

Space and time.

If there's a concept of time and space and gravity,

then there must be one for everything else.

For all the pain,

there must be an explanation.

Or for the horrific things that happen,

especially to really good people.

If You Want

If you ever wonder,

I do remember.

If you ever assume,

I don't mind the memories.

If you want me to hear you,

turn the speakers up.

If you ever have the chance to question,

I would not change a thing.

If you ask,

they won't know what I feel.

If you question,

they don't know how I felt.

If you did your best,

I always gave it my all.

If you want me back,

time takes care of itself.

There Are Times

A peak.

I think there are times,

when maybe you get a little glimpse.

Just something that starts slowly to make sense.

More often than not though, it just hurts for a while.

You have to feel the whole plot of it.

Soak it up, and feel what everything is like.

If time after time you hurt more and more,

the risk becomes greater that you won't stop.

And in that moment,

faith will do more than you possibly could.

Even if you don't believe,

something will in you.

That's the whole lesson.

Real

I guessed that around 1 million people around the world can fall in love at "first sight". I assumed in order for someone to truly consider somebody a lover, they must first go through some type of an initiation and go through things. In no way can a relationship remain simply perfect, continuously. Problems and hardships occur. There are no words that can be shared by two people to describe how someone feels. A majority of things and feelings do not actually have words that can be used to describe them. I believe things can get lost, moments can become days we never lived and too much is overlooked. That's the point of it, not having someone who expects an answer to everything. Too much of what goes on between two people is what is not said. There are the glances, the grasps, and the gestures. You have to be with someone who can read you. So that when you make slight changes, they catch them by surprise. So that you won't lose your breath trying to pipe out miscellaneous words, so that moments can be with them and so that your mind can be connected to them extremely well. If there were ways to express love, I'm positive it would be fluid, and things would never become misinterpreted. Small things would matter more, if we would let them be.

Up, Up

I wanted to snort cocaine with the man of my dreams. I wanted to be at one with the center of his mind. We counted more and more, becoming each other's alter egos. We were making insane stories through which we would throttle time in. The snowflakes made me dizzy, and then I felt like I knew what people meant about pure ecstasy. The only surface I knew better than the street was my own two plastic feet. I could walk for miles on my bitten toes. For the remainder of me was undoubtedly obscene. Nevertheless, I slowly felt the ointment of my vertebrae slithering off the calluses of my brain. It reminded me of the woman I needed to amount to being. But screw that, I'm not anymore that person than the next CIA agent. Forcing myself through trap doors… Only to be more trapped. It then occurred to me that the necklace I wanted to brand my face into already had my presence about it. And I screamed. That was my right. They are always taking me away from myself. Things don't work that way, like a lava lamp. I fall into minuscule cells, group together and make massive pieces of toxins. To make everyone think, because I don't need to. I am a child of broadened skeletal mass that envelopes the esophagus I speak to you through. I glow with intelligence. As I swim with the other angel fish.

But sharks... Oh what a pity, I die too.

Decipher

I couldn't tell you what hurts more or what shines less. What I do know is that the human heart, in itself, is flawed and magnificent to a tee. I do not know of a love that does not compromise of give and take. Nor do I have any way of telling the time between mindlessness and simple banter. We grant, we must grant ourselves the opportunity to be enough without another human gratifying and showing that to us. The world won't tell of the worth in a footstep, or the meaning your presence has in somebody else's life, but that is the joke alone. We aren't even here, not living at least. Majority of the time the mind just hurts along with the heart and the god of any light cannot merely take a pain away forever until you deal with and actually face it. Maybe you loved or simply you lost… Or a person won't describe places you've been. It could be in you. There are the struggles that ruminate in your skin and breathe, all alone. There you go around and bathe in the essence of anything that ever hurt anybody… I mean you can open floodgates, just remember what is yours to carry.

See

There are concepts beyond this world and the entire universe. There are concepts between good and evil. There is a concept of distance between which we are and who we think we are. Evidently, there is no proximity toward or away from the things we say and what we mean to say. If words had souls, numerous would be dead and buried each day, taken back and refrained. So much that people say, is said without intention or care.

As I believe that concepts are born and concepts are determined by situation, situations build perception. Without one thing happening, my whole idea of life would have been different and I would see things differently. For instance, I'm guessing that your first love either sets you up for the rest of the beauty in the world or shows you all of the pain, so that you know better where to find the beauty.

Anatomy of

Sometimes you just do, without thinking, fall in love with an idea or a mask. Maybe even a fabrication of reality. The best way to put it is that the things that we love become us and are easily our passions. To draw, to bake, to inhabit one's deepest fears, to help those in need. Maybe even you yearn to work at a hospital, giving the bad news to somebody about their loved one. To what we love, we give up the fears. That is because we must give in to the unknown. Any love is taken as a letting go, of fear.

Give And Take

You do for people, you give yourself away. Without always waiting for anything to come back to you, then you lose it. Maybe it is a loss, but maybe it is a gift. Just knowing, even if you didn't expect it, that you were able to provide somebody with parts of you that you didn't know were there. They'll live with that and you'll live with the better parts of you coming back each day. You'll grow it all back and gain a new you. You can leave the past with hopes that it won't hurt you. And it won't.

Precautions

You may love.

Release when necessary.

Let yourself lose what is meant to be lost,

it will come back

in another form.

when best needed.

Don't stall,

do the right problems on your days off.

Only answer the questions

you need answers to.

Do the world the favors it does you.

Let yourself go into new places.

Dig deep,

and come up for air.

Always swim with the sharks,

the nurse sharks, that is.

Step on the cold stones.

Water down all fire.

Believe what you can.

Love what you may.

Further the creations that belong to you.

Come back higher than you were before.

Judge only what you know you really can.

Do the dirty work yourself.

Eliminate bad people.

Forgive while you can.

Give and give,

ask for returns and ask for

what you need.

Move on from hurt,

so that it will manifest good.

All Is Pain and Love

There is no degree or term or usage for something as solid as real commitment. I don't believe you can simply teach someone to love another person. Likewise, there are no solid words or phrases to correctly encompass a beautiful relationship. How do you tell a person in a few sentences how somebody has taken all of the parts of you and embraced them wholeheartedly? When you become close enough with another human to let out all of the quirks that are beyond an exterior, something becomes golden and memorable about that experience and that person. It's so simple to forget the mortality and common ground that brings up for everyone. We all do the same basic things in order to forget the mortality and common ground that brings up for everyone. We all do the same basic things in order to maintain life. The ritualistic way of getting yourself to actually fall asleep, or the momentary lapse of time we all take before admitting anything. Commonality lies in each realm of consciousness and the connector for anybody is where they go when they have the time. There are times when you are all alone, with your thoughts and with your body. I bet it would hurt you to maintain a straight face in relaying events of your life, or while straightening out the regrets that you have. I guessed long ago that pain can only be measured on one scale and no one pound or ounce is heavier than other accounts. It just is that there is no determining factor to who endured what, it is best out of best and a guess can't get you very far. It's who you can feel out and see what they are. The luck of seeing and meeting another soul who has the capacity to feel for you, as well as themselves is ironic and rare. I found the soul of someone who knew hurt, who knew hell and gave me heaven.

For that, words are endlessly unable to reach my mouth.

Luck of the draw, I now know why the pain is relative, it is also healing and a gift to give others perhaps what you did not receive.

95

Twist

When I am walking around, I almost forget that my mind is my steady pedestal. And my body is linked to me, only partially. Half of me knows myself. The other half means nothing. This kind of resembles the world. Most people don't want the chocolate part of an Oreo, they want the vanilla or vice versa. Usually against odds, you find yourself almost alone in what you believe. Even if that is not necessarily true. We assume we aren't the same as the people around us. So we almost rule them out, what if instead we took the chances to find all our opposites. Would they still be our opposites?

How it Should Be

Down, and down,

spiraling out of control.

Tell me the beauty in that,

I don't exactly have words

to emphasize

the hypocrisy

the modern-day

glamorization

of being scared and beautiful

with glassy eyes and blood red wrists.

Or glasses of alcohol piled into a tower

it's some idea

that being in a bad state, makes you more desirable.

Because being saved is better than

having your mate, your love brings out

the already positive, good parts of you.

If there is beauty in pain,

it is that it makes us all humane

and relative to another.

It doesn't make us these sad,

characterized people like in the movies.

Because when it touches you,

outside of yourself, but in your life

and immediate circle,

it will only look like a movie when

you are dealing with the shock.

Then it hurts,

to watch it or lose them to the process.

It's overdone, and dramatic.

But in all honesty,

the glamour is not real.

On the other hand the physical and emotional pain,

that is real.

And that is what is not supposed to have glory.

But overcoming and becoming,

becoming that light,

that deserves all of the glory.

Widely spread or not,

healing is beautiful and that is what needs to be talked about.

Short Stories

In All Theory or Theoretically Speaking

There may already be that twinkle of Smirnoff on your breath the night it happens. You will have passed the remote to a faithful newcomer and me, in the kitchen laughing with a rickety smile; we will have no intention of drifting outside of that wooded interior. My eyes glossed with innocence and loaded with a lack of primal superstition. You on the other hand, a mindless part-time alcoholic, will have it all planned. Yet only half of the storyboard includes you. It's merely about everyone else. You have all of them to a tee. I can imagine the sparkle in your eyes as you turn the sides of your lips up at the proudest whore in the room. She'd lead a double life with telephone receipts dating back to the first time she asked her parents to sell her back her room or borrow money. You'd crinkle an eyebrow at the scumbag who has majored in everything but moral importance and self-worth. You'd crack your knuckle at the sight of the beautiful mother who had been everywhere but next to you. She worked herself out, and would still remain your inspiration. You'd have adapted her addictive personality though. I had done the same, with my father.

You will have already made an entrance and smoked three or four cigarettes and downed a few beers by the first hour. I will have denied my own tipsy manner.

"You alright? Dazing huh?" some friend would ask me. I'd agree and nod my head. Pulling my hair to the other side and rearranging the part, I'd look around the room. Some guy would look at me and we'd maintain eye contact until I looked away.

You will be nowhere near me. You'd probably be trying to escape the influx of young college freshman girls. When anyone our age would walk up, you'd find a way-out of their reach. Yet if they are older, you'd flock to them. Like something you had always done.

My head will spin and spin until I stumble to the bathroom and smirk in the mirror at my droopy eyes and crappy eyeliner faintly stained across my cheeks.

Being inadequate to wear a bustier, I'd opt for an old timey, but sexy and flattering dress that makes my waist tiny or something.

As I walk out of the bathroom I will see an old friend and as we talk I will remember exactly why we were no longer friends.

Then I'd realize you were there. Probably because of the smell of heavy cologne and I'd try to find where you are. Without any intention of wanting to talk or catch up, I would search for you, casually of course. And it would take me a while.

When I do find you though, you'd be playing chess.

"Wait," you'd say as I sat down across from you at the bar table in the corner of the living room.

I'd ignore you.

"You… You're," you'd stumble until I sighed sadly and told you my name.

"I remember," you'd say while getting up.

I'd move back in my seat, slowly thinking of the times I had actually spent with you and how badly I'd worked on blocking them out. The floodgates would open up the moment you would look me in the eyes and sit in front of me. I'd act calm and look at my cup and take a sip of a stupid bud light.

"Wait," you'd be drunker than a skunk, "Do you remember me?"

I waited. As you'd had said twice already.

"You look the same, the beard's coming in," I'd say.

You'd laugh.

"It is definitely," you'd say while stroking it. Then in that moment I would remember what I had really come there to remember.

It was the first time I had seen you shave your beard; I'd stayed at your place the night before and woken up in a rut. I'd walked out of your room, more confused than I should have been and I'd had a little too many the night before. You just laughed at me and walked over to kiss my forehead. I went to get cereal and came back to find you in your room but you were in the bathroom. You were pulling your hair back off your face and just using water to pull it back, you looked rugged and I loved it. It was the fantasy and love I had for grunge and Kurt Cobain probably. I remember you turning to me and singing a lyric from All Apologies I think it was. I laughed and stuffed my face with cereal. I looked up again and you were shaving and I just kept looking, at your face and the focus you took with not cutting your face. I liked the structure and features you had and. I was just enamored to see something as simple as that daily routine, I just liked it. I thought about your life outside of me and how close we had gotten and had to walk out of the room from there. I turned on the TV, dazing out and you came in about five minutes after. We sat and cuddled for hours and I found my nest in your couch, holding my butt and my head on your lap.

We broke up 3 months to that day.

"Sorry I'll go if you want me to, I just," you'd looked around and then looking down sadly," I thought we should catch up maybe".

I wouldn't know what to say. So much would come back to me.

"Actually no, I really do want to."

You'd smile.

New but Not Better

But he saw her and knew. That night had made a new person of her. I think everybody noticed the difference. Like a drop of colored paint in white, she had blended herself into a new shade; she mixed herself and became foreign. New breeds tend to try to take territory and she had failed in this. She was a lost puppy and didn't understand. He loved how she didn't see anything for how it really was though and he knew her, so very well. I remember meeting her once. She had a red stained shirt and Levi's on. Yet she still looked nice and somewhat regal almost.

"You're Ellice… I saw you at the outpatient center last week!" I said and she smiled at me while holding out her hand.

"Yeah, that was me," she said as I shivered while hearing her voice and feeling her touch. I had heard so many stories about her and now I finally was meeting her. She had these long, lilac nails and it made me jealous.

"Why were you there..." I asked, while already knowing the answer. I probably shouldn't have asked, but I needed to keep conversation. That is especially because it was a conversation of depth.

"My dad needed heart surgery, so I volunteered to drive him over here and just ended up kind of hanging out at the hospital for a while. Weird, I know" she said nervously.

I laughed.

"No, I would probably do the same thing. I'm sorry though," I said with an actually caring voice.

I saw this look in her eyes and thought instantly of what it meant but shut the thought out.

She smiled at me with all her teeth showing.

"Shit hit the fan with my family long ago, don't apologize for that," she said while laughing.

I wish I had not laughed too. But I did, which I deeply regret. I wish I would have known.

I wish I would have had more knowledge about the extent of her depression or how deeply she had fallen into drugs. I guess the whole idea of her just made me overwhelmed. She came off so strong, but she was also such an undeniably beautiful mess. She reminded me of a character in a book or a movie, but I learned that those characters don't always have the chance for happy endings like the ones we make up for book characters or movie stars.

She just was sad and I should have, I really should have, done something.

Melodramatic

He was the classic player. The kind that got any girl he wanted, even ripe out of college, he had this ego about him. Maybe he thought it was all that he had going for him and it was a type of superpower. Regardless of what it actually was, he had scarred a lot of people. He made them feel like they were worthless and of no power.

"Oh look at you," he would say to me if I looked nice one day.

I'd respond by saying, "You already did, go find someone else to gawk at."

I think he got a kick out of how blunt and almost rude I would be to him. Even to his face.

Everything had seemed to go how he had expected it to most of his life.

Up until his second year after graduating college I would see him driving around town and jamming pop music, until the day after New Years last year.

It had been months since I had seen him,when I finally ran into him at a bar. The Lazy Raccoon or something, it was a weird name.

I sat down right next to him; he turned to me and closed his eyes.

"I know this may sound far-fetched but I'm glad you're here." He said this so slowly that I was taken aback, he was serious.

"Okay I'm not going to risk sleeping with or even dating you-"

"No no, I meant just… it's good. I mean to see you, everyone around me seems so caught up in making me feel like everything is better than it is. You just put off a casual vibe and you don't get what everyone else seems to think is good about me."

109

"You are not good," I said while ordering a rum runner from the middle aged waiter, "I did go to college with you. I can't tell you how many girls cried to me about you, my lord, I bet some have your name on their graves." I said.

He laughed and sort of looked down.

"I was not good. You are right." He acknowledged.

"Why, what was the point?" I asked.

"I think a part of me felt that it was my only control. I was stable in knowing that at least attracting women and then hurting them left me with power. It's not cool, I regret it, but I think it gave me something. Something beyond the chaos." He said, as I stared intently at him wondering what I had just heard.

"Tell me your chaos, I'm sure you already know mine" I said referring to my stints in rehab, because of alcohol and bipolar disorder.

"Simple, my mom believed in physically reprimanding my sister and I and my dad didn't really mind it. He just wanted to make sure I wasn't a closet gay like him. Wow I don't know why I am telling you my life story, I apologize…" He said.

"Oh hell no, don't go there. I didn't even know… Wow. I would say I'm sorry but I don't believe sorry does anything really."

"It's funny because it doesn't, but thank you. I guess being around you feels good because you are one of the only women in this town that I never felt I had to make amends with to even feel comfortable enough around." He said this while looking right into my eyes.

I smirked.

"I see where you are coming from." I said.

"I think I needed to be around someone who finally didn't know me too well, and you don't really. Or at least you didn't really," he said.

"That's fair. Let's do this. Tell me something."

"Alright," he said turning all the way to me.

"Describe yourself in one word," I said while sipping the last of my drink.

He waited.

"Independent"

I gave him a nod of approval.

"And you?" he said to me.

I laughed and put a finger up to represent that I needed a minute.

I coughed.

"Reliant." I said.

Misunderstanding

When I initially began, my head just spun around the idea. I had to understand, to comprehend, why anybody was capable of mutilating themselves and in turn, becoming a story. From what I knew, books were the only places I wanted to hear stories. I had assumed that nobody would desire to leave this life with a legacy so negative and promiscuous. I mean promiscuous in life, somebody who was alright with teetering on both realms. There was a concept of adultery with mortality I had thought. Now, I believe that there is almost a jolt that comes from knowing that you are right in the middle ground. I began to see so much sadness but also so much understanding in the people. I couldn't exactly describe why they had such a wise quality until I was able to comprehend it all.

"You chose to… Why?" I asked.

"I knew that I was in school… I was just learning… Lesson after lesson, on a bigger scale and I had gotten to a point where I didn't want to anymore. I was just done with it. So I accepted that there are things I won't learn and downed a bottle of Xanax."

I just sat there for a very long time.

"What if you decided, just theoretically, to become the teacher?" I wondered aloud.

The beautiful brunette looked to me and laughed while wiping her thick bangs out of her eyes.

"I did," she said.

If the Ground Does Break

It was years after I had anticipated the meeting to be. My hands were sweating and I was anxious. It was the kind of fear that resonates in the pit of one's stomach and travels through the body. I had already thought about what I was going to say, and then I remembered that it would come out nowhere near how I would want it to.

I knew that I would have to tell my counselor about everything, all of it. There were so many things I really could not talk about and that was simply out of memory loss. I had not relapsed and I was positive in knowing that I wouldn't. But for my story to seem accurate I would have to be more convincing. No, I hadn't fallen in love or found myself again. Instead, I had finally seen what I was and realized that it was far from where I had pictured.

"You look good," she said.

"I got a few highlights and put some blush on," I said while laughing and moving forward to hug her.

Mal was beautiful and not in a way that you would describe as attractive. She was beautiful in what emanated from her soul and from her voice, she had an angelic voice.

"It's good to see you." I said this sincerely, because unlike the last time I had seen her, I was not lying. Her smile widened and she sat down across from me.

We were at this really cute coffee shop, the kind that they use in movies. Not the real high budget movies but the small-town kind that tugs at your heart strings and ends happily for every character. I laughed quietly to myself as I saw a young girl walk by with her mom and ask if she could get another coffee cake. She whined when her mom pulled her away from the counter.

"I bet you were like that," Mal motioned to the girl and her mom, "feisty I'd imagine."

I cracked a smile.

"I was, I wanted everything and especially at that age. My mom was given a hand full with me" I joked.

"I was the same way oddly enough," Mal said.

We both knew there was more we needed to talk about. There was business to be done.

"So how are you, you know physically?" Mal asked.

"I'm, I'm good. I workout a lot and try to eat well," I noticed her staring at me, "I am sober."

We both took a second and just looked at the other.

When I had been in the facility Mal was my go-to. She was great and she knew everything about how detox affected the body but also the mind. I would talk to her each day and I grew close to her. There was so much about my personal life that I wanted to share with her but I refrained because I knew that it would be unprofessional.

"That's great to hear Grace," she said while smiling ear to ear.

"I know I was supposed to write to you more and probably keep you updated but when I first got out… Honestly I didn't want to remember all of it. And I don't mean you, I mean the experience. It was tough."

Mal instantly looked down and seemed upset.

"You were probably one of the most dedicated," she laughed and turned her head to the side to look at a cute waiter, "but also caring people I had ever worked with and I knew it would be a process to recover."

"I've found it almost beautiful… It's like a kind of rebirth and not in the way that they always say but more in how you see yourself and the world. I guess I had done so much wrong that when I did start doing right, it engulfed me."

It was a moment between when we both looked right at each other again.

"Good. That is really good. You have seen the benefits of treatment and now you are reaping them." Mal said this so contritely. I could tell she didn't want to connect with me at the moment.

"Look, I know I'm not exactly there yet but I do think that I will become what I want to be. I haven't relapsed," I said.

Mal seemed awkward and upset.

"I have," Mal said quick like it was nothing.

Instantly I lost all of my train of thought.

I whispered the word 'what'.

"I uh, yeah I did."

I hadn't really known about Mal's past and now that I had a clue, I wanted to help. Even though I knew it could possibly be very awkward.

"Let me go with you, anywhere," I said.

"I am okay Grace, it was once," she replied back to me.

"Alright that's bull shit, we are leaving. I'm getting the tab and we are road tripping to somewhere and talking and working this out."

"I'm your counselor, you are not mine G," she said slowly.

"You told me it was important to be supportive of other addicts, that's what I am doing," I grabbed my bag and put forty dollars on the table.

"We are leaving." I said it without a hint of doubt.

It took a while to get her out of there but when we did I found a way to talk her into driving to Georgia with me. I said we would go for the Blue Ridge Mountains.

We spent two months on the run from ourselves and slowly in that we somehow found who we were. I was able to find something even better though. My entire life I had thought that there were people who had overcome the things that I hadn't and that they would always know more. Mal had overcome what I had but it came back up and in some ways that humbled me to know that I wasn't alone in vulnerability. I don't really know if I can promise that Mal won't relapse again or go back to old ways but for me, I think I like myself in nature and sober. I think I like being real and vulnerable without using a substance for the excuse to feel feelings. I am really living, with every fiber of emotion and sensation.

About the Author

Sammantha Rials was born in Valencia, California and moved to Bradenton, Florida at the age of four. She is currently a student at Lakewood Ranch High School and is the Associate Editor for her school's journalism department.

Sammantha intends on taking her passion for writing and direct it towards a major in Broadcast Journalism when she goes to college. Her goal is to give a voice to the unheard and bring a compassionate and honest expression to all the stories she shares.

www.ingramcontent.com/pod-product-compliance
Lightning Source LLC
LaVergne TN
LVHW011207080426
835508LV00007B/651